Early Recovery

(Poems from an Alcoholic)

Noah B. Wheeler

To Mom, Dad, Sydney and Dakota
Thank you for everything

Contents:

Acknowledgements:

This collection would not have been possible without the support and encouragement from Jaquie, John, Cassandra, Mandy, and all of my friends made along the way in recovery. Words cannot express my gratitude for everything you have done to show me a new way of life, my life is immeasurably better because you have been in it. To my parents, thank you for your unending support and love through all of my endeavors. Sydney, you always seem to call when I could use a distraction and never fail to deliver. To my sponsor, thank you for talking me off the ledge and always having time for me. Dakota, you are my best friend and make me feel like it's okay to be myself, your support and love are the reason I'm able to share this much of myself with the world. Thank you so much!

My Path

The path I walk is winding
Tangled strings dragging in my wake
Debris collecting, a crushing weight
Quick-sand would be faster
This journey into darkness
Aided by my drunken harness

The path I walk is winding
Further from the truth I go
The ending is not happy
That's the truth I know
I have all the answers
In my diluted mind
The one I always turn to
Will kill me in its time

The path I walk is winding
My spirit, body, mind in pain
A tiny spark of hope appears
I see another way
The path that once was winding
Is not the path for me

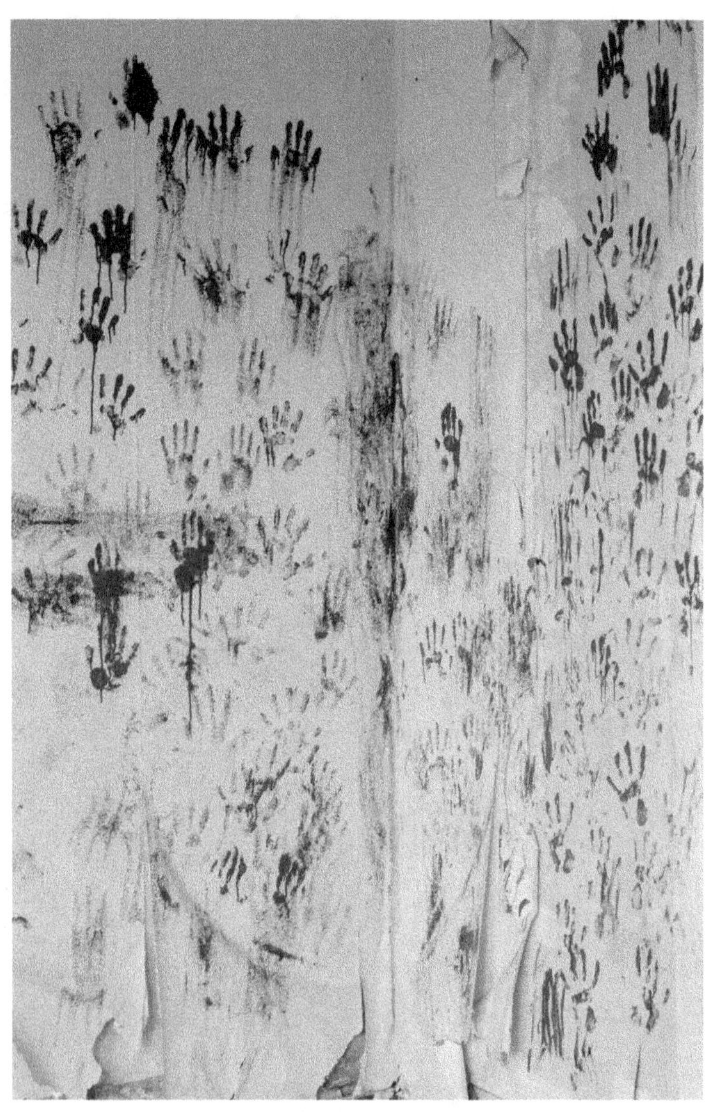

Death

The medicine I've chosen
Will not cure my disease
The problem is not the answer
Though it appears to be

I take my daily dosage
Or two or three or ten
My broken brain repeating
The pain will finally end

I sit alone in darkness
Surrounded by false friends
For they don't truly know me
And I do not know them

We hoist our liquid savior
We say a toast and cheers
A brief charade of happiness
Takes all that we hold dear

It's not a problem, trust me
I tell to those who care
Though I can't look them in the eye
It's death at whom I stare

I Sit

I sit inside an endless darkness
The shadows hide the key
I cannot see beyond the veil
Of pain and misery
Disease infects my thoughts forever
The choice no longer mine to make
Tell myself it's almost over
Though I know that I will break

I sit inside an endless darkness
Blind to what's outside
No escaping from this prison
I've created in my mind
Mistakes, missteps, and errors
Playing on repeat
Looking to the scoreboard
I see that I've been beat

I sit inside an endless darkness
Counting down the days
The weeks turn into months and years
An everlasting stay
No parachute upon my back
The lifeboat is going down
I'm captain of this sinking ship
This is my time to drown

Hello Me

With this pen I put to paper
All the feelings in my heart
A jumbled mess inside me
Can't tell them all apart

The hurricane is raging
The levees all are breached
Drowning in obscured emotions
Myself I now must meet

An awkward introduction
Put off for far too long
This small talk only shows me
How disconnected I've become

Traces of remembrance
Flashes there and here
But I don't recognize this man
Reflecting in the mirror

The fog is slowly lifting
A vague shape starts to form
A ray of sunlight shining through
My chance to be reborn

And though I don't yet know the way
I trust in those who guide me
For my path lead into the dark
And now the sun is rising

My Journey

Where do I wander?
What path will I take?
My hands reaching out, but both feet in the grave

I've been down the road
Of potholes and rubbole
Debris and detritus, each mile a struggle

Each bump a reminder
Each crack a relapse
Each pebble as sharp as a knife in my back

But I see a fork
A chance to break free
This new road is maintained, fresh swept it's kept clean

I'm turning the wheel
Each foot a new story
It's only the start of my recovery journey

Armor

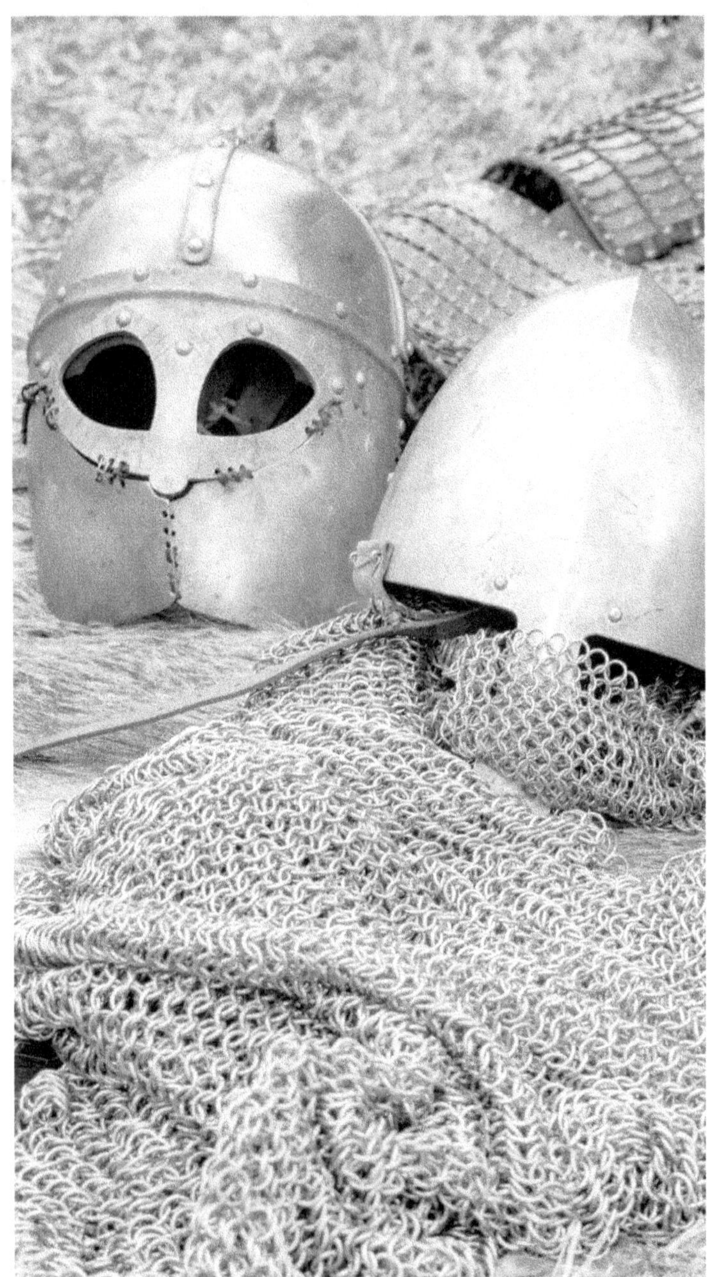

I dress in suits of armor
Standing tall for all to see
Glimmering and shining
Exuding gallantry
But within the helm and chestpiece
Where sunlight cannot reach
A vast unyielding darkness spreads
Like storms upon a beach

I dress in suits of armor
I smile, laugh, and grin
But I can't seem to find the words
To share what lies within
Emotions too ambiguous
These feelings aren't defined
I need to find a codex
To decipher my own mind

I dress in suits of armor
To mask what lies beneath
Searching through this labyrinth
That no one else can see
I open up my mouth to speak
But only air departs
Help me take the chain mail off
So I might bare my heart

WEATHER

Darkness is a rain cloud
Rolling through the sky
Anxiety is thunder
Ringing out on high
Cravings are the lightening
Blinding with its flash
Depression is the tidal wave
Engulfing every path
Anger is the hurricane
A devastating rage
Shame lies in the raindrops
And dampens every page
Guilt is the humidity
Heavy in the air
But pain is just a lack of tools for when the weather's there

Rain with an umbrella
Is a meditative beat
And thunder's just a warning
Of the storm that we will meet
Lightening sometimes shows the path
When we have lost our way
And tidal waves rejuvenate
A once forgotten bay
Hurricanes bring crushing ruin
But rebuilding makes us strong
We can't control the weather, but we can rewrite the song

Time

Time has no friend
It leaves us in its wake
It leaves us trembling
It leaves us reaching
It leaves us reeling
It leaves us feeling all these feelings
It leaves us begging for more
It leaves us wishing to go back
It leaves us desperate and alone
It leaves us yearning for the past
It leaves us disconnected
It leaves us an afterthought
It leaves us fucked up in the head
In the end it leaves us dead
Time has no friend

Stars

Stars fly in the night
Bright and fast
Dark and slow
Some twinkle and barely move
Other blaze across the sky
They all have their time and place
And leave a mark upon my eye
The imprints fade with time
When I gaze up I see memories
Of gleaming galaxies
Black holes of empires long past
Showers of light
Raining down
Some I'll see once in my life
Others return night after night
They all become a part of me
As long as I remember

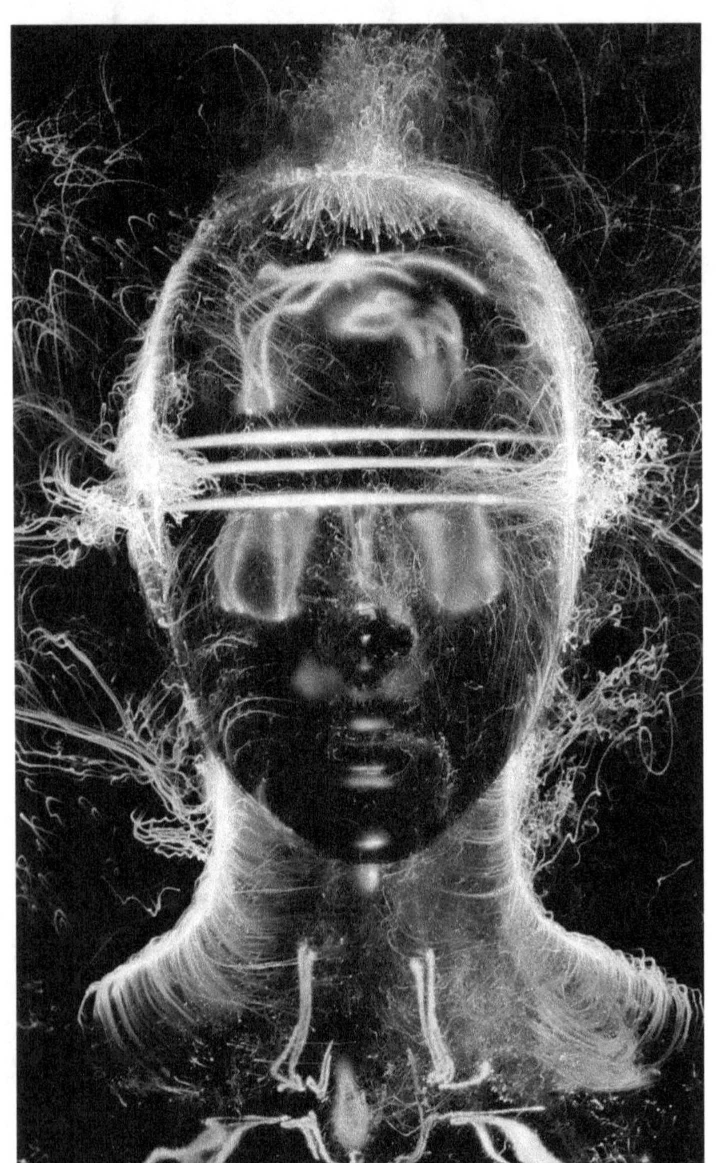

My Weapon

This isn't anger or rage
That's too easy
One punch
Throw shit
Satisfy the angst

This feeling is deeper, stronger
It grows when I hide
This sadness and frustration
Can't change what I can't change
I still try, sometimes
A fight that wasn't mine
I still put on the gloves
Swinging
But the target is too far

Exhaustion finds me
I bow out
Turn back to myself
To live in what I feel is my weapon
And I will hone it always

The Depths

The ocean is the story
A perfect allegory
With depths beyond conception
I sit in contemplation
The tides will rise and fall
But never do they stall
The highs bring great elation
And lows a dark sensation
Deep crevices and trenches
Where sunlight never reaches
But life remains existent
Instinctual persistence
Though natural light is absent
A glowing aura's present
When creatures live so deep
Do they even need to sleep?
When day and night are synonym
And no circadian rhythm
I live inside my own self
But still call out for help
And when I'm lost within the reef
My friends will show me to the beach

Disease in Me

Is this enabling?
I shake my head and think
Is it so bad to take another shot or drink?

It's only sparingly
I keep it on a leash
But one misstep and this addiction's dragging me

Now I can't even sleep
I counted every sheep
It's in my head controlling everything I think

I'm clinging to my sheets
And crawling shakily
I try to stop but this disease won't let me be

This drunken life I lead
Can't let my family see
Cause I can't stand it when I hear my mama weep

To be or not to be
This isn't poetry
It's how I'm chasing to by lying six feet deep

Emotions baffle me
It's getting hard to breath
I can't get help because I lie in therapy

Do I live evilly?
Sometimes I drive and drink
I crashed into a car and made a minor bleed

But I'm still in one piece
It haunts my every dream
Would it be better for the world if I deceased?

Dark Seas

Darkness in the tide
It ebbs and flows
The waxing moon controls my mind

Desolate sands
A tomb so vast
Decaying whales and crabs reside

Footprints never last
Nor castles
Figments of this bleak mandala

Sunlight wanes
The shadows rule
Death's hand within my grasp

Look out to sea
Crashing waves
Crippling as I try to stand

Gravity
A crushing weight
My smile masks the misery

Rise again
To no avail
Anchored to a sinking ship

No screams
No wails
A chorus of the deepest trench

Echoes die
Without the air
Trapped by nothing everywhere

Manic

These wild swings
The hardest test
The voice inside me heckles
Exuberance and glee abound
One second
Not the next
Cling to joy
Remain content
My demon won't allow it
Just a taste
From time to time
To amplify the sadness
I joke and laugh
Throughout the day
My levity is known
Bring smiles to the ones you love
So they don't watch you drown

Fucked Up

My mind's pretty fucked up
But I can't even say that's just me
When I don't know who I'm supposed to be
Don't even know who I am
Am I a man?
Am I a boy, lost with no plan?
I'm an enigma
A riddle not meant to be solved
Looked in the mirror don't know what I saw
I am a stranger
Inside of my head I'm in danger
So many monsters and scars
Their teeth and their claws
Tearing me down while they're ripping me up
I need a bump
I need a shot or a tab or a blunt
To take me away
Cause I'm stuck in this place
And I feel like I'm always making mistakes
And missteps
I keep falling down
Drank up the ocean cause I want to drown
This is the misery
This path is so slippery
And I don't know what way is up
Or what way is down
I'm beating my head on the ground
Pray for some sweet relief
Pray when I wake, these aches and these pains
Won't be killing me
But that's not my life

Claw at my eyes, I reach for a knife
Just to feel something, outside of my mind
The blood looks so nice
Am I so fucked up?
I think that I'm fucked up

Blood clots, the flow stops, mic drops
And now I'm back inside my head
So loud, but no crowd, bad sounds
Telling me to make it end
Can't breath, I'm too weak, there's no peace
This is an SOS my friend
Insance, I can't change, my thoughts rage
This can't be real I must be dead

Help Me

This heart's not meant to heal
And the pain too much to feel
So many shards inside my chest
And I can't fix this mess

A bullet would be faster
Wine more dignified
A rope would be poetic
But all paths lead to death
I'm trying not to give up
I'm trying to stay strong
But every move I make
Feels like I'm doing something wrong

The pills would creep up slowly
A quick jump from the roof
Or cut myself wide open
Cause I can't stand the truth
I'm trying to keep going
I try to move along
I try to make it better
By singing this sad song

I'll hold on just one more day
My promise to myself
Tomorrow start it over
And try to find some help

CRAVINGS

CRAVINGS HIT AROUND THE CLOCK
EVERY TIME I WANT TO STOP
I GO TO POUR THE LIQUOR OUT
NOT DOWN THE DRAIN BUT IN MY MOUTH

THE LIQUOR LAUGHS AS IT'S DEPLETED
ONCE AGAIN I HAVE BEEN CHEATED
THIS EVIL COURSING THROUGH MY VEINS
AM I DISEASED OR JUST INSANE?

THERE'S NO RELIEF
I SCREAM AND SHOUT
THIS SUBSTANCE I CAN'T LIVE WITHOUT
IT COMES TO ME DRESSED IN DISGUISES
WHAT IT OFFERS TANTALIZES

THE SUN IS FADING
LIGHTS GO OUT
WHERE THE FUCK DID I PASS OUT?
WAKE UP
LIGHTS ARE DAGGER SHARP
MEMORIES ARE TORN APART

IF I CAN'T STOP I WON'T SURVIVE
I MUST REPAIR THIS BROKEN LIFE
ONE DAY AT A TIME, I PRAY
TO MAKE THESE DEMONS GO AWAY

Cravings II

Can't stop these cravings
I'm going crazy
Can't catch a break
When they hit me on the daily
I share at meeting
And go to therapy
But the voice inside my head
It's always pressuring

Just one sip, just one shot
Just one puff, why'd you stop?
One to five and five to ten
Lost my count it's time to binge
I hear last call, those awful words
Two more shots to hit the road
Turn the key cause I'm just fine
This is how I always drive

Wake up still behind the wheel
My car won't move or even steer
My chest is bruised and feet are sore
Can't even open up my door
Cops roll up with flashing lights
Here to lock me up tonight
Failing tests and blowing high
Now the end is fucking nigh

Still Alive

This is what we always did
I was just a normal kid
Hanging out after school
Acting stupuid with my friends

Staying up on all the trends
Emo hair and jeans slim
Stomping, looking scary
In my Doc Martens

Now look at who we emulate
What they smoke and what they drank
Can't be cool without a substance
Shooting through your veins

Drinking codeine Lil Wayne
Smoking dank, Snoop and Dre
Swimming pool full of liquor
This is how you play the game

But I was never seeking fame
Didn't care about my name
I just want to be accepted
And embraced for a change

But it's harder than you think
When you try but only sink
Medicating this depression
With another fucking drink

This ain't a video game
Can't respawn and replay
Take the lessons learned the hard way
Turn them into a gain
Cause it's not pleasure it's pain
I put both feet in my grave

I played dumb games won dumb prizes
It's a surprise I'm alive and
I still got chances to thrive and
I won't look back on my life and
Regret the choices that I made
Because they put me where I'm at

And now my living is clean
And now I'm living my dream
Sobriety reminds me that life is
So full of meaning

My last dollar bill
Burning in my right pocket
Should save but I drink

Staggering blindly
The bar is my only sight
My heaven my hell

The door is ajar
Walk through the shadows and live
My fight will go on

Where is the bottom?
Have I already seen it?
Or still going down?

The tape is wound back
The past is written in stone
Today a new story